Macmillan/McGraw-Hill Science
Energy and You

Take Me To St. Louis

AUTHORS

Mary Atwater
The University of Georgia

Prentice Baptiste
University of Houston

Lucy Daniel
Rutherford County Schools

Jay Hackett
University of Northern Colorado

Richard Moyer
University of Michigan, Dearborn

Carol Takemoto
Los Angeles Unified School District

Nancy Wilson
Sacramento Unified School District

Macmillan/McGraw-Hill School Publishing Company
New York   Chicago   Columbus

Take Me to St. Louis

Themes:
Energy / Systems and Interactions

Lessons

Activities!

EXPLORE

TRY THIS

Fiber optic strands

What Happened in 1904?

October 7, 1904

I can hardly believe I am on a train to St. Louis with my family. We are on our way to the World's Fair. My mother said, "Kathleen Brown, it is too late in the day for you to be writing in that old book. The sun is setting and the train is dimly lit. You will harm your eyes!"

I told her I have to write in my journal every time I get excited about something new. I guess she understands.

3

I can't believe what I see in the distance. It is night and the city is as bright as if it were day. How could this be? Father said St. Louis is lit with gaslights instead of candles and kerosene. I can see Cousin Elizabeth!

When we got to my cousin's house, we played shadow tag in the brightness of the gaslights. I jumped on Elizabeth's shadow six times.

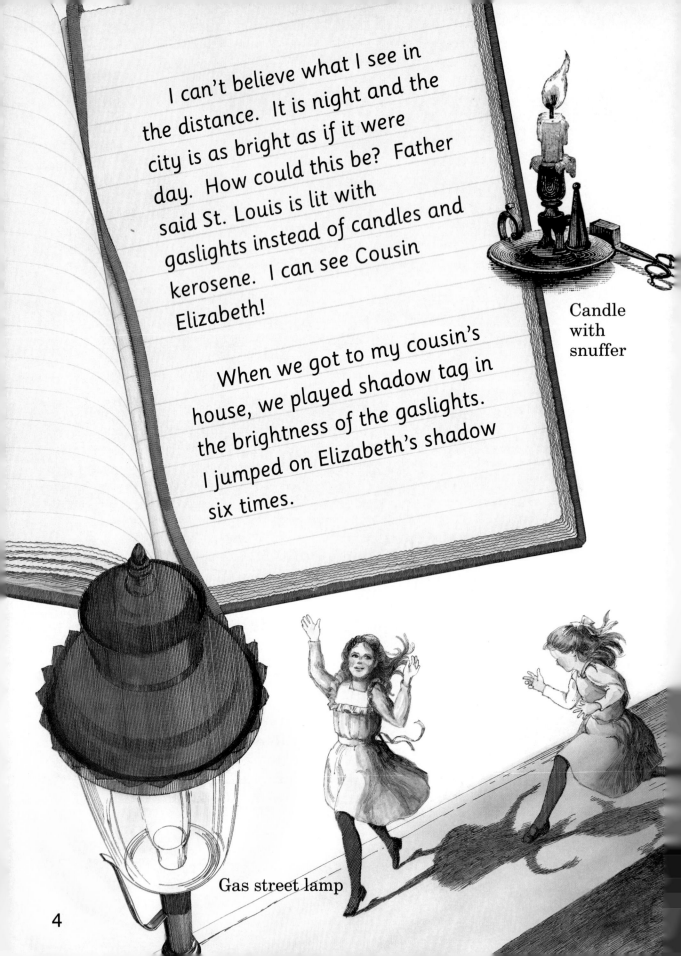

Candle with snuffer

Gas street lamp

4

Minds On! Name all the sources of light Kathleen saw. What other sources of light do we use now? ●

Gas street lamp and lamplighter

Activity!

Lights **and Shadows**

Why do you think Kathleen was excited to play shadow tag at night? When do you see shadows? What would you need to make shadows? How do shadows change?

What You Need

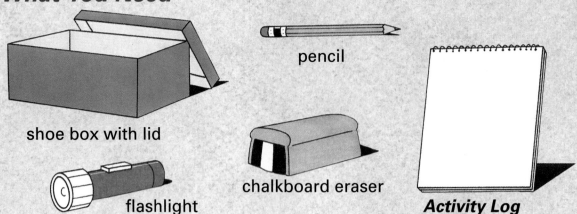

shoe box with lid

pencil

chalkboard eraser

flashlight

Activity Log

What To Do

1. Make a peephole in the box with the point of the pencil.

2. Place the eraser inside the box. Put the lid on the box.

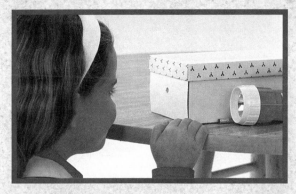

3. Look into the box through the peephole. What do you see? Do you see the eraser? Do you see its shadow?

4. Make another peephole in the lid of the box with the pencil.

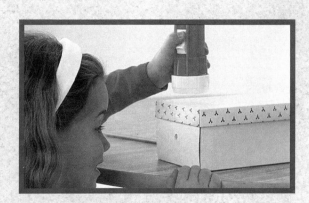

5. Look into the box while you shine the flashlight through the top. What do you observe? What is different with the light?

What Happened?

1. Describe in your *Activity Log* what you saw the first time you looked into the box.

2. What do you think makes it possible to see objects?

3. What made it possible for Kathleen and Elizabeth to see as they played at night?

4. What made their shadows appear?

EXPLORE

A Day at the Fair

October 8, 1904

The sunbeams in my face woke me up! Today is going to be my first day at the World's Fair. I am staring at the sunbeams as I wait for someone else to wake up.

I wonder what time it is. At home we get up at sunrise. City folks seem to stay up later at night than we do. Gaslights make it easier to see at night than our candles.

Elizabeth just blinked open her eyes. I am glad she is awake. I can't wait to get to the fair.

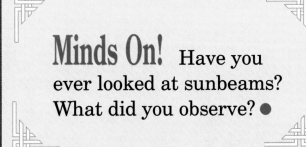

Minds On! Have you ever looked at sunbeams? What did you observe? ●

Activity! *Light Beams*

What You Need

flashlight
2 chalky erasers
Activity Log

Darken the room. Have a partner hold a flashlight and shine a beam of light toward a wall. Clap the erasers together into the beam. What do you observe? How does this remind you of sunbeams? What do you see in sunbeams? Tell about it in your *Activity Log.*

When we arrived at the fair there were so many buildings, people, parades, and lights. There was a Ferris wheel that could hold 60 people in every car! Every building was lit up. Cousin Conrad said a man named Thomas Edison showed people how to use electric light bulbs instead of gaslights.

Inventor, *Thomas A. Edison*

CAREERS

Thomas Edison was a famous **inventor.** He worked with a group of people to improve the electric light bulb. He also helped to make moving pictures and phonographs. What do you think makes someone a good inventor?

11

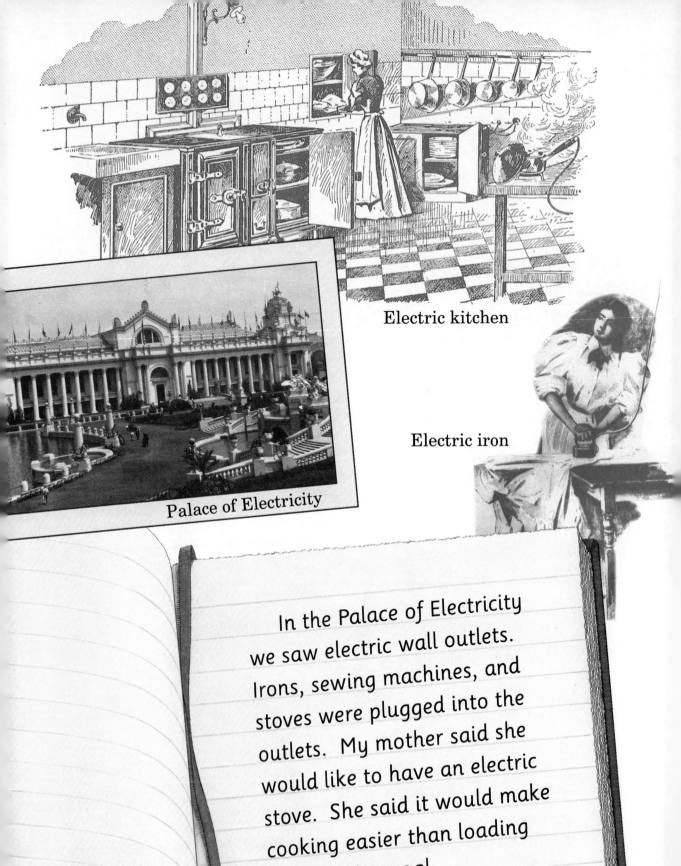

Electric kitchen

Electric iron

Palace of Electricity

In the Palace of Electricity we saw electric wall outlets. Irons, sewing machines, and stoves were plugged into the outlets. My mother said she would like to have an electric stove. She said it would make cooking easier than loading and burning coal.

Think about each **invention** on this page. Why do you think each one was made? Not all inventions use electricity. Can you think of one that does not? Can you think of something that still needs to be invented?

Electric sewing machine

Edison light bulb

TRY THIS 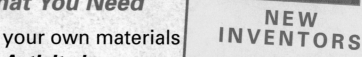 **Activity!**

WANTED!

NEW INVENTORS

What You Need

your own materials
Activity Log

What can you invent that might solve a problem or make work easier? What do you need to make your invention? Gather some materials and try putting your invention together. Record what you do in your *Activity Log.* Draw a picture of your invention and tell how it works.

Photographer

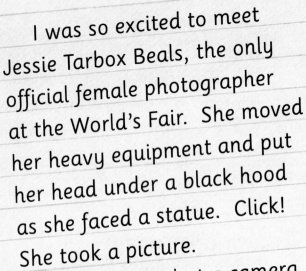

I was so excited to meet Jessie Tarbox Beals, the only official female photographer at the World's Fair. She moved her heavy equipment and put her head under a black hood as she faced a statue. Click! She took a picture.

She told us that a camera cannot work without light. She said that it must be perfectly dark inside the box. I know now that her camera lets in some light but only for an instant, when she clicks the shutter.

Your eyes work like cameras. Light comes into one part of the eye and reaches the lens. The lens turns the picture of what you see upside down. Parts of the body called nerves send the picture to the brain. The brain turns the picture right side up and tells you what you see. As you do the next activity, try to find out how a camera is like your eye.

lens

14

TRY THIS

Make a Pinhole Camera

What You Need

2 empty soup cans,
  both ends cut out
waxed paper
rubber band
masking tape
black poster board
pushpin

black construction paper
Activity Log

What To Do

1. Trace around the end of one can onto the black poster board. Cut around the circle leaving 1 cm of space between the circle you've drawn and the line you're cutting.

2. Tape the black circle to the end of one can leaving the center of the circle clear of tape. This is now can A.

3. Punch a hole in the center of the black circle with the pushpin.

4. Cut a piece of waxed paper large enough to completely cover the opposite end of can A. Hold it in place with the rubber band. Be sure the waxed paper is tight.

5. Tape one end of can B to the waxed paper end of can A.

6. Wrap a piece of black construction paper around the two cans and hold it in place with tape.

7. Go outside in the bright sunlight. Cover your head with something dark, like a jacket. Ask your partner to stand about 2 m in front of the camera and wave his or her arms up and down. What do you observe? Which part of your camera is the lens? How is a camera like your eye?

The Pike

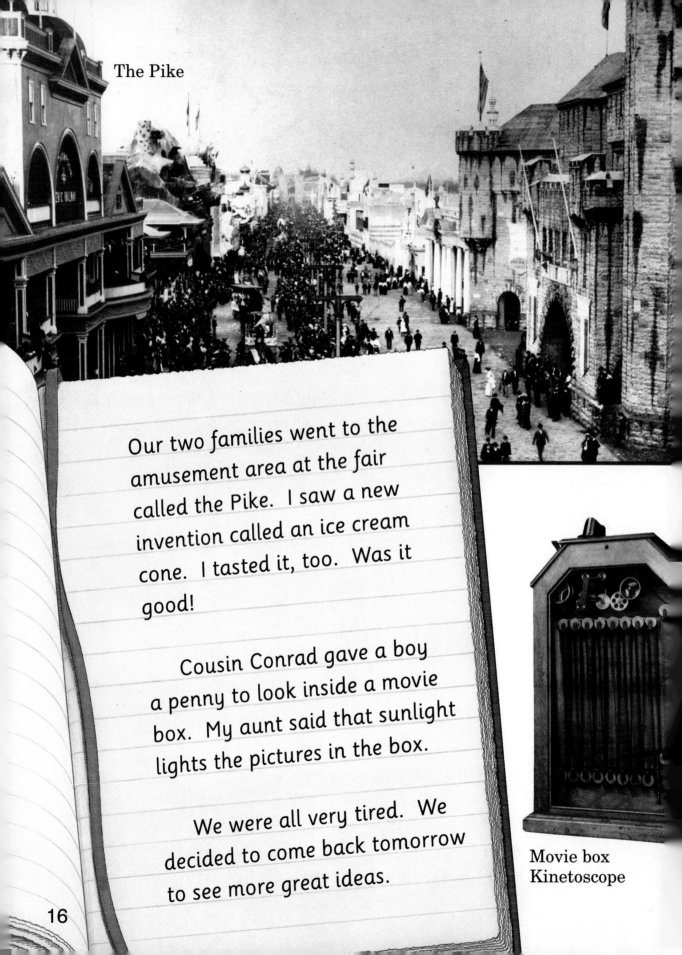

Our two families went to the amusement area at the fair called the Pike. I saw a new invention called an ice cream cone. I tasted it, too. Was it good!

Cousin Conrad gave a boy a penny to look inside a movie box. My aunt said that sunlight lights the pictures in the box.

We were all very tired. We decided to come back tomorrow to see more great ideas.

Movie box
Kinetoscope

Discovered at the World's Fair!

A vendor ran out of paper dishes to serve his ice cream. He asked the baker next to him if he could use some of the baker's waffles. He wrapped the waffles around his ice cream. Can you guess what happened next?

As people visited the 1904 World's Fair they saw many new and different things. How did the discovery above and the invention below change people's lives?

Activity!

The Zoetrope: A Movie Machine

What You Need

    flashlight
    record player
    oaktag movie machine
    Activity Log

Set the movie machine your teacher has made onto the turntable. Turn on the record player at its slowest speed. Shine the flashlight through the slots. What do you see? How do you think this invention led to something new?

I can't fall asleep even though the room is dark. I keep thinking about everything I saw today that made or needed light . . . the new electric lights, the camera, the movie box.

Mother came in a while ago to kiss me goodnight. Her shadow filled the room. I could see the gaslights on the wall in the hall behind her. When she left—so did her shadow. I think I know why.

I asked mother to leave the door opened a little so that I could write in my journal. What a wonderful day I had!

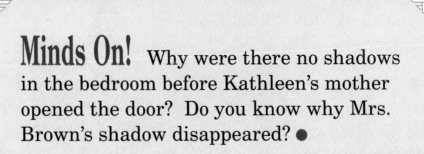

Minds On! Why were there no shadows in the bedroom before Kathleen's mother opened the door? Do you know why Mrs. Brown's shadow disappeared? ●

What do you think about the World's Fair of 1904? It must have been very exciting for Kathleen and others to see so many new inventions all at once.

Our times are exciting, too. People work to invent new things every day. How do you think old time inventions led to the inventions of today?

Zoetrope

Video camera

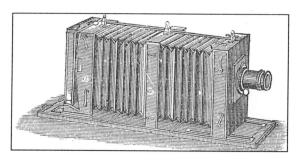

Bellows camera

Camera of today

Gas street light

Highway lights

What Can You Find Out About Light?

When people think of an idea to improve something or invent something new they often follow a plan. First, they predict what might happen if they tried their idea. Then, they observe what happens when they experiment. They record their observations. They experiment over and over again to see if the same thing happens every time.

Thomas Edison's laboratory

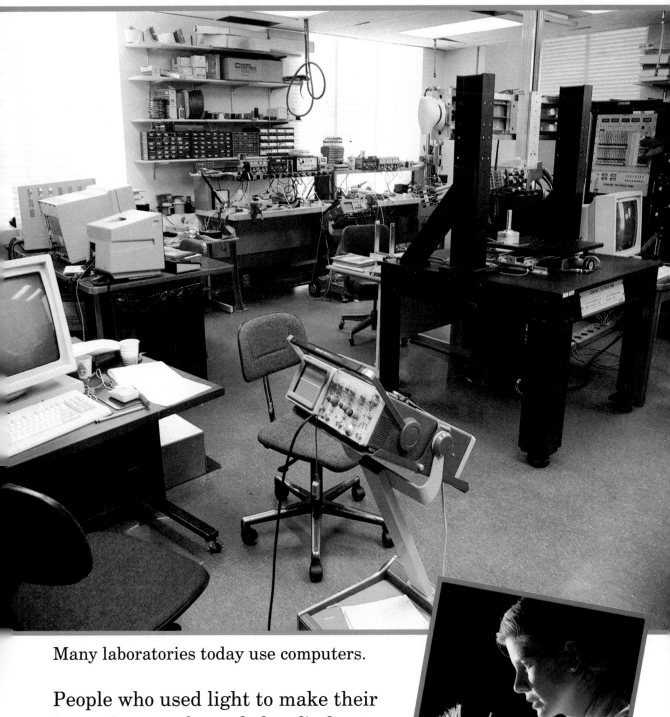

Many laboratories today use computers.

People who used light to make their inventions work needed to find out about light. They needed to observe how light behaved. Suppose you need to find out about light. Do the experiment on the next page to see what you can find out.

Fiber optics—a new way to use light

Activity!

How Does Light Travel?

What do you already know about light? Did you remember that you cannot see anything without light? Did you think about how shadows are made? What else can you find out?

What You Need

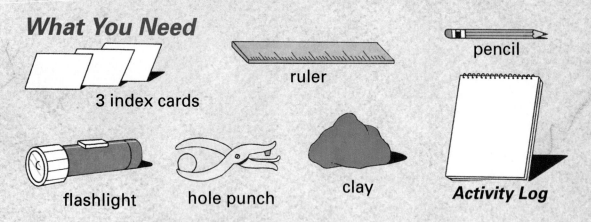

3 index cards

ruler

pencil

flashlight

hole punch

clay

Activity Log

What To Do

1. Use your ruler to draw lines on each card from one corner to another to make an X.

2. Punch a hole in each card where the lines cross.

3. Stand the cards up in the balls of clay. Space the cards about 15 cm apart one behind the other, so that you can see straight through the holes.

4. Ask a partner to shine a ray of light straight into the first hole. What do you see the light do?

5. Have your partner shine the light into the hole from the side. What do you see the light do?

6. Move the cards so that you cannot see straight through the holes. Try the light again and see what happens.

What Happened?

1. What changed when you moved the cards? Write what you think in your *Activity Log.*

2. How did you make the light travel through the holes in all three cards at the same time?

3. What did you find out about light?

EXPLORE

23

What Is Light?

Did you find out that light travels in a straight line? Just like sound and heat, light is in motion. Light is the way **energy** gets from the sun to Earth. Sunlight is the main source of energy for Earth. Every living thing on Earth depends on light from the sun. Can you think how?

Even though the sun is far away in space, it only takes about eight minutes for light from the sun to reach Earth. It travels to Earth in straight lines.

Minds On! Work with a partner to think of things other than the sun that are sources of light. Make a list of them. ●

25

To See or Not To See

Most objects do not make their own light. But some objects allow light to pass through. Can you think of some?

A few objects allow some light to pass through.

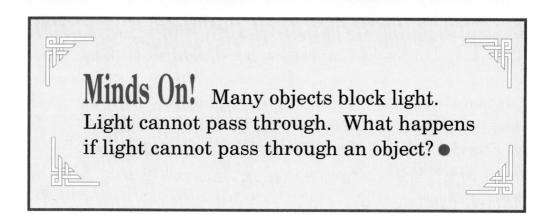

Minds On! Many objects block light. Light cannot pass through. What happens if light cannot pass through an object? ●

What materials might make the best windows? Do the Try This Activity and find out.

Window Watching?

What You Need

construction paper	scissors	waxed paper
brown paper bag	typing paper	plastic wrap
cooking oil	flashlight	tape

Activity Log

Make a house shape with five cut-out windows. Make one square each of waxed paper, plastic wrap, and typing paper. Make two squares of brown paper. Make each square a little bigger than your cut-out windows. Pour a little oil on one square of brown paper. Tape the squares onto the window shapes. Shine the flashlight through each one. Which squares make the best windows? Why?

How Do We See Most Objects?

You learned in the Explore Activity on pages 6 and 7 that it is not possible to see anything without light. If most objects block light, and they do not make their own light, how do we see them? Do the Try This Activity to find out.

TRY THIS

Activity!

Please Pass the Light!

What You Need

flashlights   mirrors
Activity Log

Work with a partner. Darken the room except for one bright light. Each person first "catches" light in a mirror and bounces it onto a wall. Try it again. This time have your partner try to "catch" your beam of light with his or her mirror and then bounce it onto a wall. What is happening to the light? Make some notes in your *Activity Log* about the game.

Objects like mirrors are smooth and shiny. You can see how they **reflect** light. Light rays hit them and bounce off. They bounce off in only one direction.

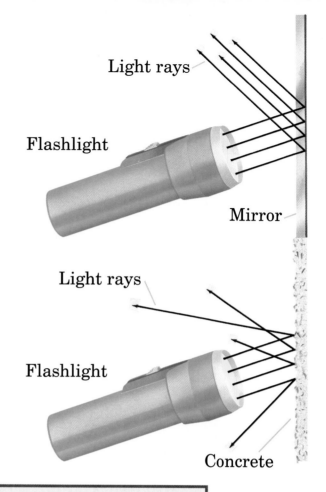

Light rays

Flashlight

Mirror

Objects that are not smooth reflect light, too. The light rays that hit them bounce off in many directions.

Light rays

Flashlight

Concrete

Minds On! Find objects in your classroom that reflect light easily. How are these objects alike? Write about the objects you find in your *Activity Log.* ●

Inventions That Use Light

As people began to understand light, they figured out how they could use it. They invented many instruments that used mirrors to reflect light.

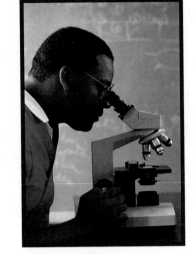

When you look through a lens on a microscope, objects look bigger than they really are. You must use light to see through the lens. Some microscopes use mirrors to reflect light.

Microscope

A telescope allows you to use light to make objects that are far away look closer.

Telescope

A periscope is used in a submarine. Some periscopes have mirrors that reflect light off each other. It allows you to see objects above the surface when the submarine is underwater.

Submarine periscope

Do the next activity to find out how a periscope uses light.

Activity!

Up Periscope!

What You Need

shoe box
2 nonbreakable mirrors
2 cardboard strips (28 cm x 5 cm)
masking tape   scissors
Activity Log

What To Do

1. Tape each mirror in the middle of each cardboard strip. Do not cover up the mirror with the tape.

2. Tape the cardboard strips in opposite corners of the shoe box. Be sure each piece of cardboard is taped tightly to the sides of the box.

3. Use your scissors to cut two holes in the box. Cut them directly across from each mirror. The holes should be about as wide as a stick of gum.

4. Put the lid on the box. Hold the box upright in your hand and peek through one of the holes. What do you observe?

Write about it in your **Activity Log**. What did you make?

The 1904 World's Fair introduced many new inventions. A lot of the inventions made then and since use energy from light. Which invention do you think is most important?

Glossary/Index